DISCARD

Bucket Trucks

by Derek Zobel

BELLWETHER MEDIA • MINNEAPOLIS, MN

Note to Librarians, Teachers, and Parents:

Blastoff! Readers are carefully developed by literacy experts and combine standards-based content with developmentally appropriate text.

Level 1 provides the most support through repetition of high-frequency words, light text, predictable sentence patterns, and strong visual support.

Level 2 offers early readers a bit more challenge through varied simple sentences, increased text load, and less repetition of high-frequency words.

Level 3 advances early-fluent readers toward fluency through increased text and concept load, less reliance on visuals, longer sentences, and more literary language.

Level 4 builds reading stamina by providing more text per page, increased use of punctuation, greater variation in sentence patterns, and increasingly challenging vocabulary.

Level 5 encourages children to move from "learning to read" to "reading to learn" by providing even more text, varied writing styles, and less familiar topics.

Whichever book is right for your reader, Blastoff! Readers are the perfect books to build confidence and encourage a love of reading that will last a lifetime!

This edition first published in 2009 by Bellwether Media, Inc.

No part of this publication may be reproduced in whole or in part without written permission of the publisher. For information regarding permission, write to Bellwether Media, Inc., Attention: Permissions Department, Post Office Box 19349, Minneapolis, MN 55419.

Library of Congress Cataloging-in-Publication Data
Zobel, Derek, 1983–
  Bucket trucks / by Derek Zobel.
     p. cm. – (Blastoff! readers : mighty machines)
  Includes bibliographical references and index.
  Summary: "Simple text and supportive images introduce young readers to bucket trucks. Intended for students in kindergarten through third grade"–Provided by publisher.
  ISBN-13: 978-1-60014-234-5 (hardcover : alk. paper)
  ISBN-10: 1-60014-234-6 (hardcover : alk. paper)
  1. Truck-mounted cranes–Juvenile literature. I. Title.
  TJ1363.Z63 2009
  629.225–dc22   2008033097

Contents

A **bucket** truck
is a tall machine.
It can reach
high places.

bucket

A bucket truck has a **cab**. The driver sits in the cab.

cab

A bucket truck has **legs**. Legs keep the bucket truck steady when it works.

leg

A bucket truck
has an arm.
The arm lifts
the bucket.

arm

A worker stands in the bucket. The worker uses **controls** to move the bucket.

LIFT-ALL

CVPS

plug'n go
www.cvps.com/plugngo

USDOT 347512
RUTLAND, VERMONT

The controls
can move the
bucket in any
direction.

This worker stands in a bucket to repair **power lines**.

UTILITY

17

This worker stands in a bucket to cut down a tree.

Firefighters spray water from this bucket to put out a fire! Wow!

Glossary

bucket—the part of a bucket truck where a worker stands; the bucket is at the end of the arm.

cab—the place on a vehicle where the driver sits

controls—the levers and switches that make a machine work; a worker uses the controls of a bucket truck to move the bucket.

legs—strong metal beams that come out of a bucket truck; legs keep a bucket truck steady.

power lines—thick wires that carry electricity

To Learn More

AT THE LIBRARY

Bingham, Caroline. *The Big Book of Trucks*.
New York: DK Publishing, 1999.

Blum, Mark. *Big Trucks and Diggers in 3-D*.
San Francisco, Calif.: Chronicle Books, 2001.

Rogers, Hal. *Cherry Pickers*. Chanhassen,
Minn.: Child's World, 2007.

ON THE WEB

Learning more about mighty
machines is as easy as 1, 2, 3.

1. Go to www.factsurfer.com.

2. Enter "mighty machines" into the search box.

3. Click the "Surf" button and you will see a list
   of related Web sites.

With factsurfer.com, finding more information
is just a click away.

Index

The images in this book are reproduced through the courtesy of: Jon Patton, front cover, p. 7; Allister Clark, p. 5; Bob Pool, p. 9; Rick Donovan, p. 11; Associated Press, p. 13; David Hoffman, p. 15; David H. Lewis, p. 17; Powered by Light/Alan Spencer, p. 19; Bob Carey, p. 21.